drawing for "DORKS"
& much more!

Animals

Y0-CMF-400

IMAGINE THAT

Licensed exclusively to Imagine That Publishing Ltd
Tide Mill Way, Woodbridge, Suffolk, IP12 1AP, UK
www.imaginethat.com
Copyright © 2020 Imagine That Group Ltd
All rights reserved
0 2 4 6 8 9 7 5 3 1
Manufactured in Guangdong, China

Drawing for Dorks Quiz

How much of an artistic dork are you really? Take this fun quiz to find out and discover your inner dork!

1. If I were to paint a picture it would be of...
   - [ ] a. a busy city, or great architecture.
   - [ ] b. a natural landscape, like a beach or a forest.
   - [ ] c. a wild animal.

2. If I were to create a picture quickly I would...
   - [ ] a. not rush — perfection takes time!
   - [ ] b. sketch from real life in pencil or charcoal.
   - [ ] c. take a photograph, then use it to draw a picture later.

3. If I were to visit anywhere to draw for the day, it would be...
   - [ ] a. a museum.
   - [ ] b. a forest in the mountains.
   - [ ] c. a nature reserve in another country.

4. If I were to do anything this weekend, I would...
   - [ ] a. visit a modern art gallery to see the latest pictures.
   - [ ] b. pack up my paintbrushes and get outside to draw!
   - [ ] c. stay in the studio — so many pictures to create, so little time!

If you answered...

Mostly As

You are a super-confident artistic dork! You see inspiration in everything. You know your artistic style and aren't afraid to stick to it to create art your way!

Mostly Bs

You are a super-wild artistic dork! You draw what you see and like to keep your art real, taking inspiration from nature to create beautiful pictures of natural habitats.

Mostly Cs

You are a super-creative artistic dork! You aren't afraid of a drawing challenge and know how to stay true to your art style without compromising on quality!

Drawing Smarts

Follow these useful drawing tips as you create your awesome animal works of art!

- Get comfortable! You can draw at a table, in the park, or you can even draw standing up waiting for a bus — just make sure you are comfortable before you start!

- Use a pencil to start your drawings. If you make a mistake, then you can easily erase it and start again.

- Don't worry if you do make a mistake — just remember to have fun!

- Drawing is mostly observation, so take time to study what you are drawing.

- Practice makes perfect!

Awesome Elephants

Dork facts to amaze your BFs...

⭐ Elephants are the largest land mammal in the world!

⭐ Elephants like hanging out with their friends and live in herds, often with other family members.

⭐ Elephants are herbivores (vegetarians!) and eat leaves, roots, twigs, and bamboo.

⭐ Elephant moms-to-be are pregnant for 22 months!

⭐ Elephants can recognize themselves in a mirror.

⭐ Don't feed an elephant peanuts! Elephants don't like peanuts.

 Reasons why I love elephants SO much...

_____
_____
_____
_____
_____
_____

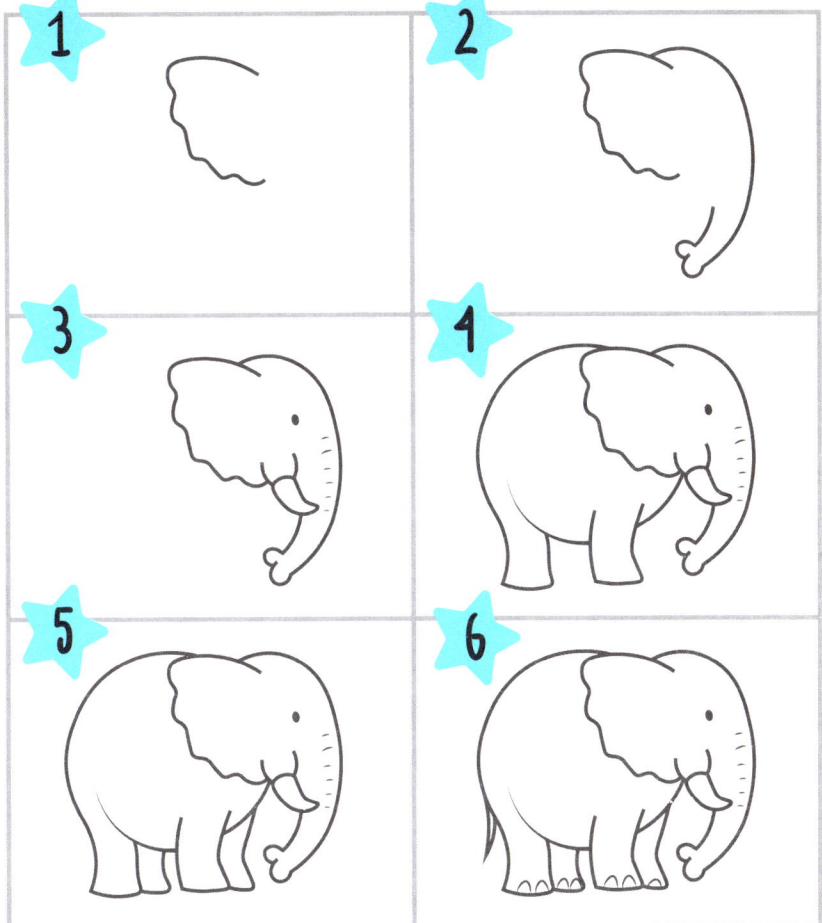

YOUR TURN!

Amazing Zebras

Dork facts to amaze your BFs...

⭐ There are three species of zebra, all native to Africa.

⭐ Zebras are similar to horses in almost every way, except for their dazzling black-and-white striped coat!

⭐ Scientists think that zebras recognize each other by their unique black-and-white stripes.

⭐ Zebras spend most of the day grazing on grass, leaves, and twigs, traveling thousands of miles to find fresh pasture.

⭐ Zebras live together in herds. Sometimes they combine with other herds to create a "super herd" of thousands of zebras!

⭐ Zebras have fierce fighting skills, using their powerful legs to kick out when under attack.

 Reasons why I love zebras SO much...

_____

_____

_____

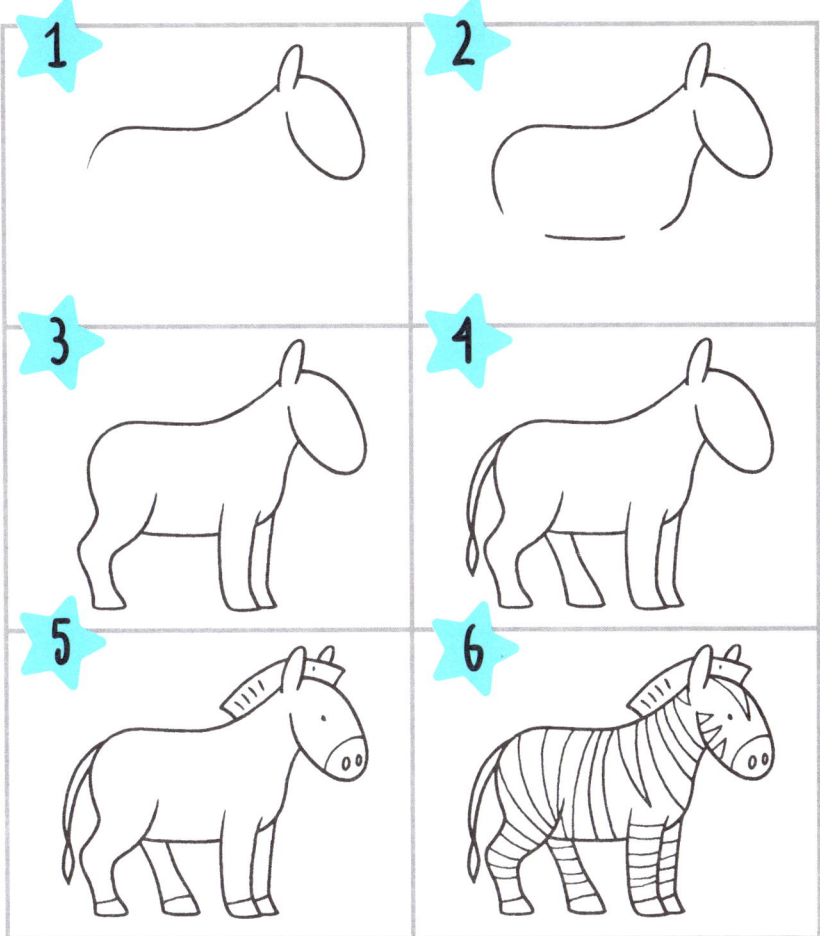

YOUR TURN!

Beautiful Bats

Dork facts to amaze your BFs...

⭐ There are over 1,300 species of bats. Some are tiny while some have wings measuring 6 feet wide!

⭐ A bat's wing is actually their hand. Their thumb and four fingers are connected to each other by skin, which acts as a wing.

⭐ All bat species around the world fall into two groups: microbats and megabats.

⭐ Microbats feed on insects at night and use echolocation to see in the dark.

⭐ Megabats are fruit-eaters and are found in hot tropical countries. They have larger eyes than microbats, but smaller ears and do not use echolocation.

⭐ All bats sleep upside down, hanging from their back legs.

 Reasons why I love bats SO much...

_____

_____

_____

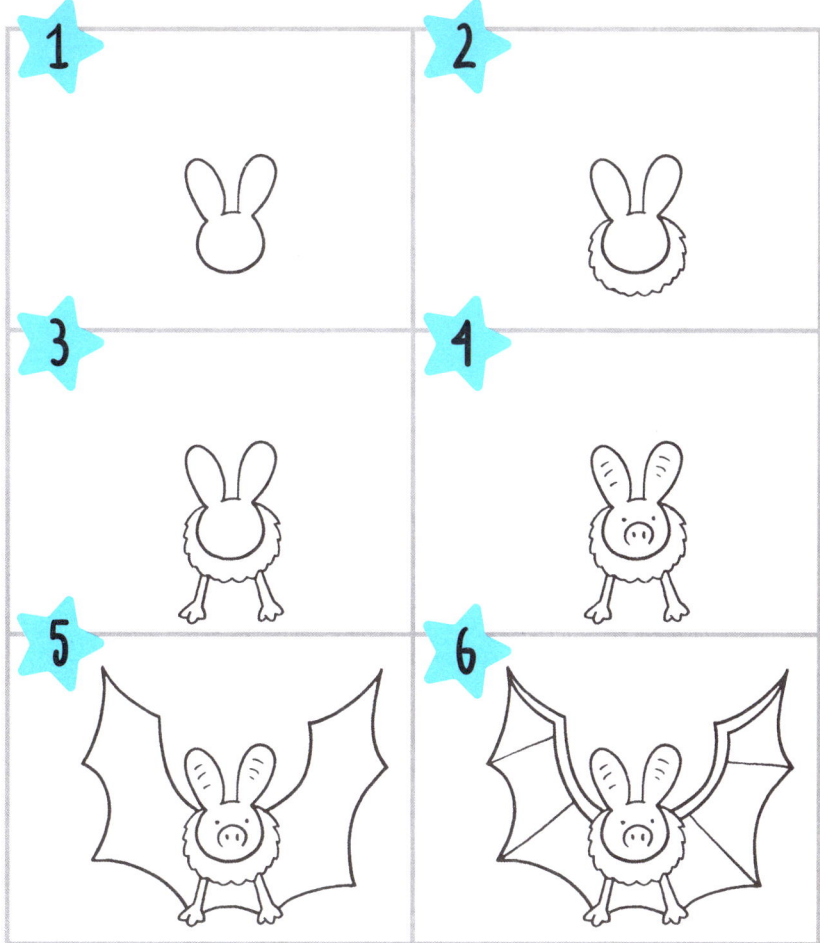

YOUR TURN!

Super Sea Turtles

Dork facts to amaze your BFs...

⭐ Turtles are found in nearly every ocean on Earth. Although they breathe air, they spend all their lives at sea.

⭐ There are seven species of sea turtle. The smallest is the Kemp's ridley, which weighs up to 100 pounds.

⭐ The largest turtle is the leatherback turtle, which can weigh up to 1,540 pounds!

⭐ Each species eats different food. Green turtles eat sea grass, leatherbacks eat jellyfish, and Kemp's ridley turtles feed on crabs.

⭐ Sea turtles have been on Earth for over 110 million years!

⭐ Sea turtles migrate thousands of miles across oceans to lay their eggs and to feed. One leatherback turtle was recorded traveling over 12,000 miles across the Pacific!

 Reasons why I love sea turtles SO much...

_____

_____

_____

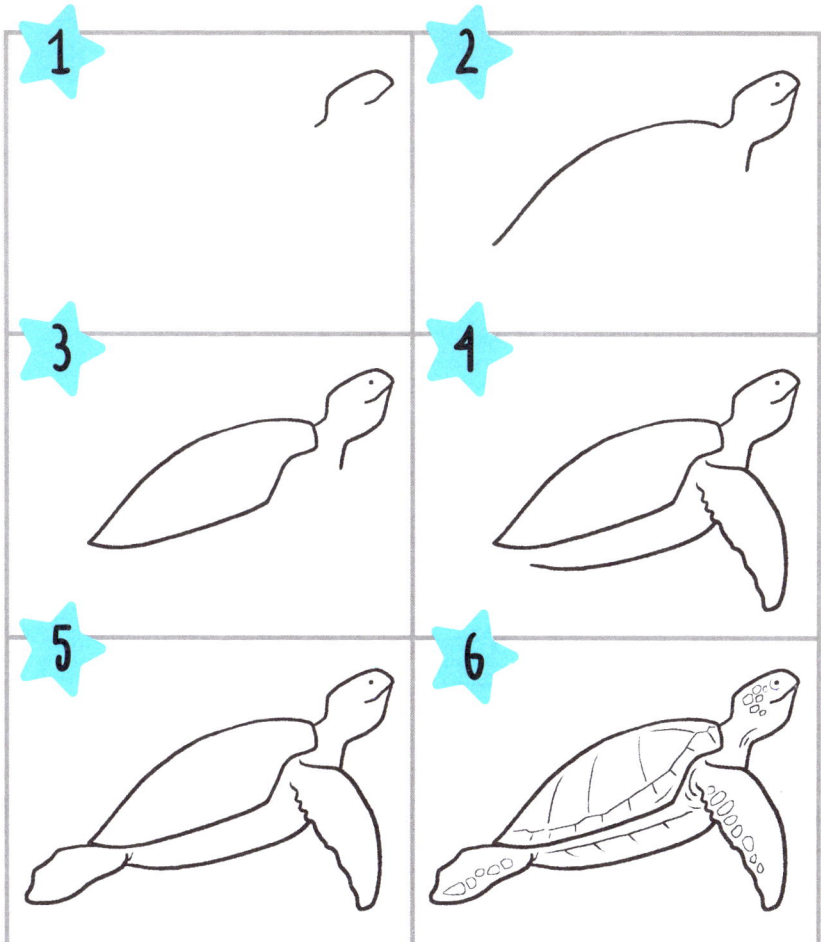

YOUR TURN!

Mighty Polar Bears

Dork facts to amaze your BFs...

⭐ Polar bears are powerful predators, found in the coldest environments of the Northern hemisphere.

⭐ Polar bears are the largest of all the bears. They are over 9 feet long and weigh up to 1,600 pounds.

⭐ Polar bears are expert swimmers. Their large webbed front paws help them paddle underwater.

⭐ Under their white fur, polar bears have black skin which soaks up warmth from the sun.

⭐ The bottom of a polar bear's paws are covered in fur. This protects against the cold and helps them to grip onto ice.

 Reasons why I love polar bears so much...

_____
_____
_____
_____

YOUR TURN!

Cool Chameleons

Dork facts to amaze your BFs...

⭐ There are over 160 species of chameleon on Earth!

⭐ Nearly half of all chameleon species are found in Madagascar. The rest are found in Southern Europe, Africa, and Asia.

⭐ Chameleons change color to communicate with each other and sometimes they change for camouflage.

⭐ Chameleons have 360° vision! Each eye can rotate separately so they can see in two directions at the same time.

⭐ To catch prey, a chameleon shoots its long tongue out from its mouth at super-quick speeds.

⭐ Chameleons feed on insects such as grasshoppers, locusts, and stick insects.

 Reasons why I love chameleons SO much...

_____

_____

_____

_____

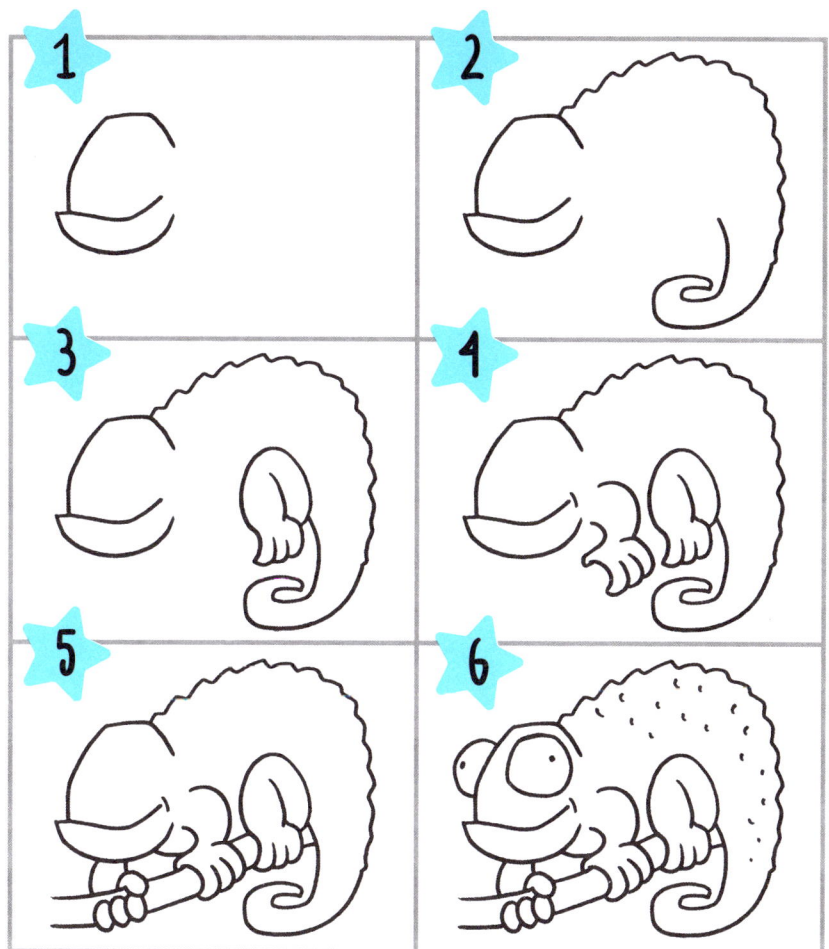

YOUR TURN!

Great Grasshoppers

Dork facts to amaze your BFs...

⭐ Famous for their songs, grasshoppers make sounds by rubbing their legs or their wings together.

⭐ Grasshoppers have five eyes! Two large eyes on each side of their head and three small eyes near their antennae.

⭐ Grasshoppers have no ears. They use special organs on their abdomens (called tympanum) to hear.

⭐ Grasshoppers are amazing jumpers. Their strong back legs mean they can jump up to 20 times their body length!

⭐ Some grasshoppers will eat any kind of plant it finds. Swarms have been known to eat entire fields of crops!

 Reasons why I love grasshoppers SO much...

_____
_____
_____
_____

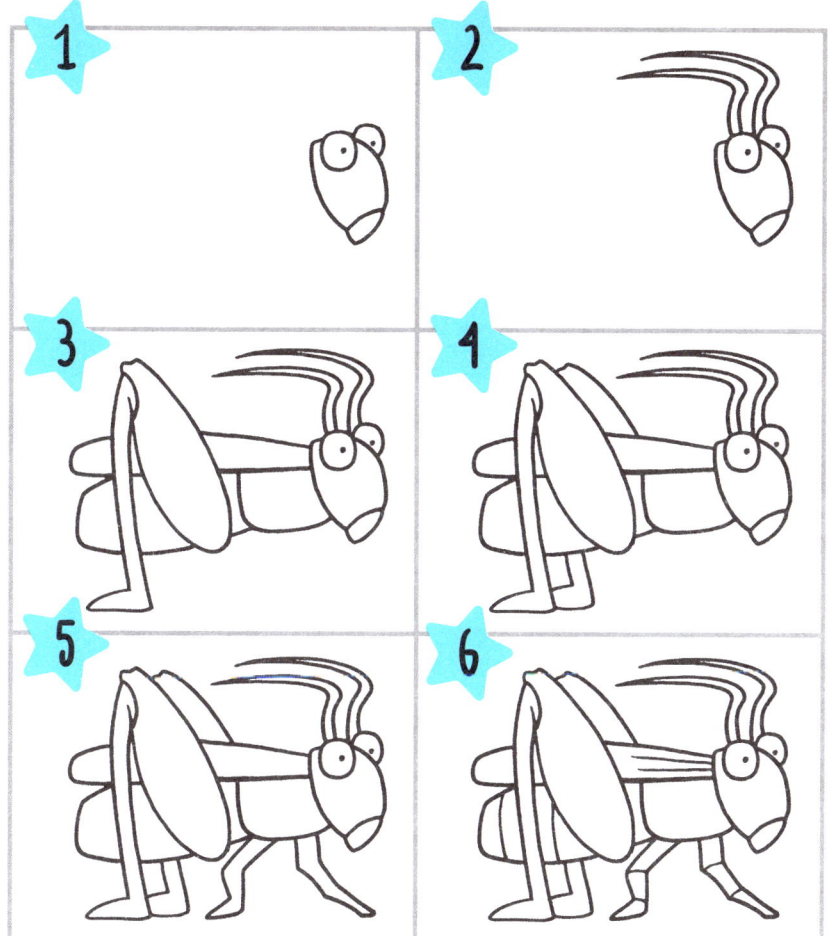

YOUR TURN!

Terrific Toucans

Dork facts to amaze your BFs...

⭐ Toucans are found in tropical rainforests in Central or South America.

⭐ There are 40 different species of toucan. They vary in size from 7 inches to over 2 feet long!

⭐ Toucans are well known for their large, colorful bill, which they use to eat fruit hanging from hard-to-reach branches.

⭐ Toucans can even use their bills to peel fruit like oranges!

⭐ A toucan's large, colorful bill can grow to 1 foot long — nearly half of their body length!

⭐ Toucans make lots of noise — their grunts and croaks sound a bit like a frog's!

 Reasons why I love toucans so much...

_____

_____

_____

_____

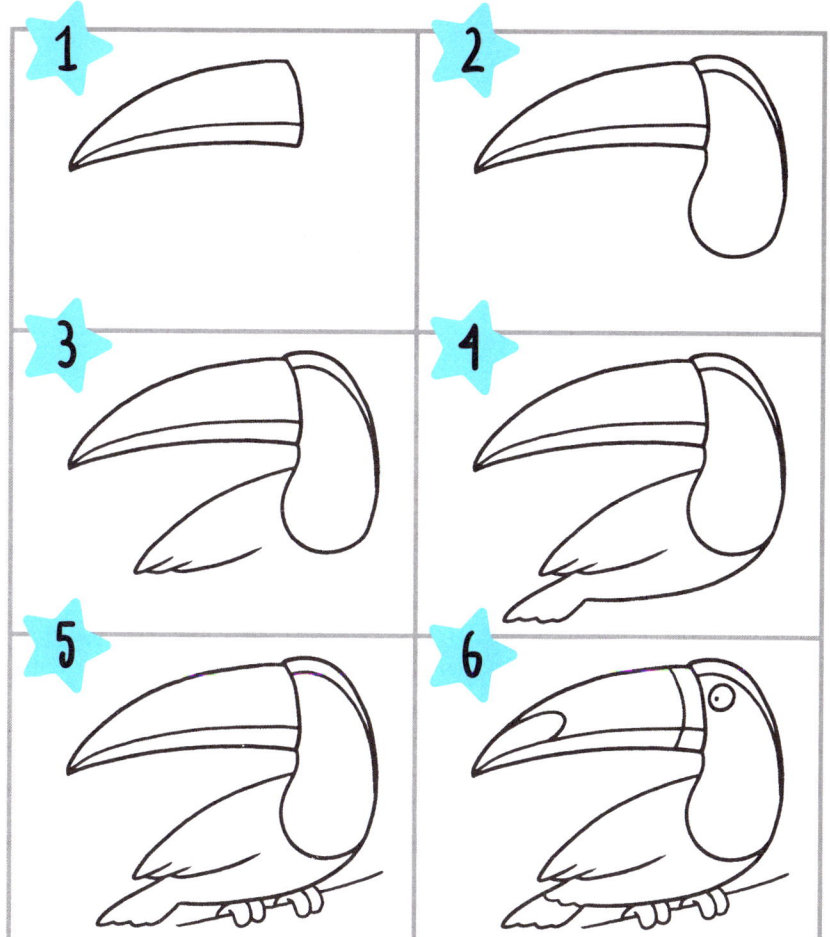

YOUR TURN!

Majestic Lions

Dork facts to amaze your BFs...

⭐ Lions live in groups called prides. Each pride contains 10 to 15 lions.

⭐ Lions are mostly found in sub-Saharan Africa, but there is a species of forest lion found in northwest India.

⭐ Female lions work together to hunt for food between dusk and dawn.

⭐ While the females are hunting, a male lion will protect the pride and patrol its territory.

⭐ An adult male lion's roar is so loud it can be heard up to 5 miles away!

⭐ The long hair around a male lion's head is called a mane.

 Reasons why I love lions so much...

_____

_____

_____

YOUR TURN!

Great White Sharks

Dork facts to amaze your BFs...

⭐ Great white sharks are found in oceans around the world and are the largest predatory fish on Earth.

⭐ The largest great white sharks measure over 20 feet long – that's longer than the average car!

⭐ With streamlined bodies and powerful tails, great white sharks can swim up to 35 miles per hour!

⭐ They have incredibly strong jaws packed with over 300 sharp teeth.

⭐ A great white shark has an amazing sense of smell! They can detect prey from over two miles away.

 Reasons why I love great white sharks SO much...

_____

_____

_____

_____

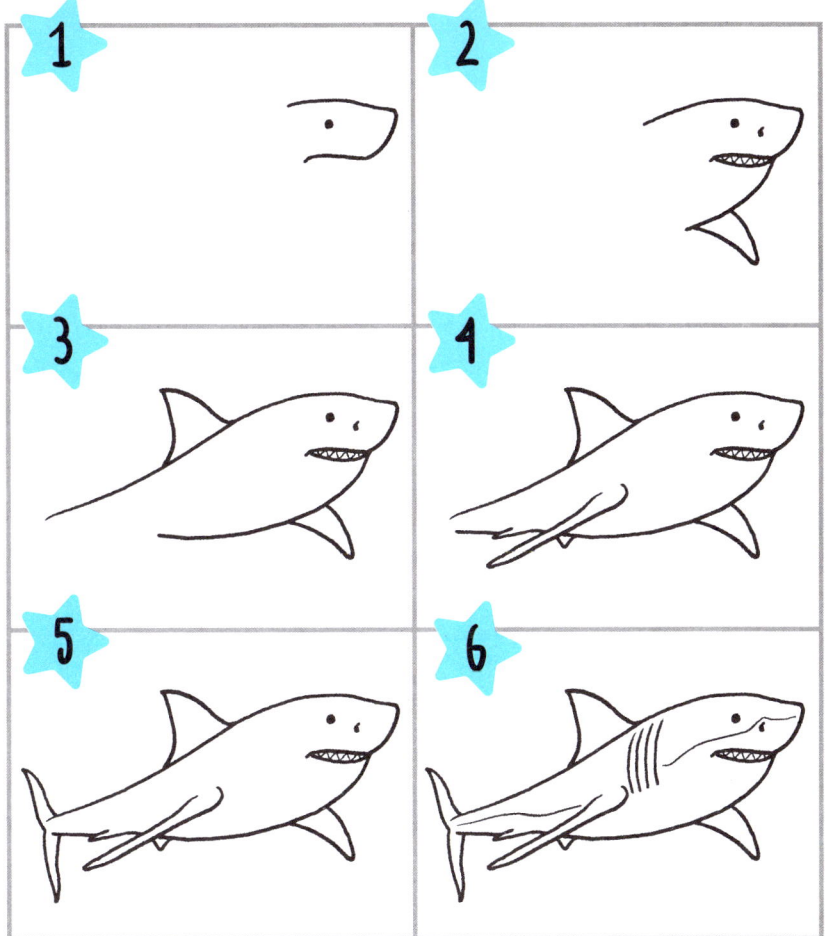

YOUR TURN!

Perfect Peacocks

Dork facts to amaze your BFs...

⭐ The large, colorful birds called peacocks are actually peafowl and are part of the pheasant family of birds.

⭐ There are three species of peafowl: the Indian, the Green, and the Congo.

⭐ Males are called peacocks, females are peahens, and baby peafowl are called peachicks.

⭐ Peacocks are best known for their beautiful long tail feathers, which can measure up to 5 feet long.

⭐ Each tail feather features an iridescent eyespot circled in bright green and bronze.

 Reasons why I love peacocks so much...

_____

_____

_____

_____

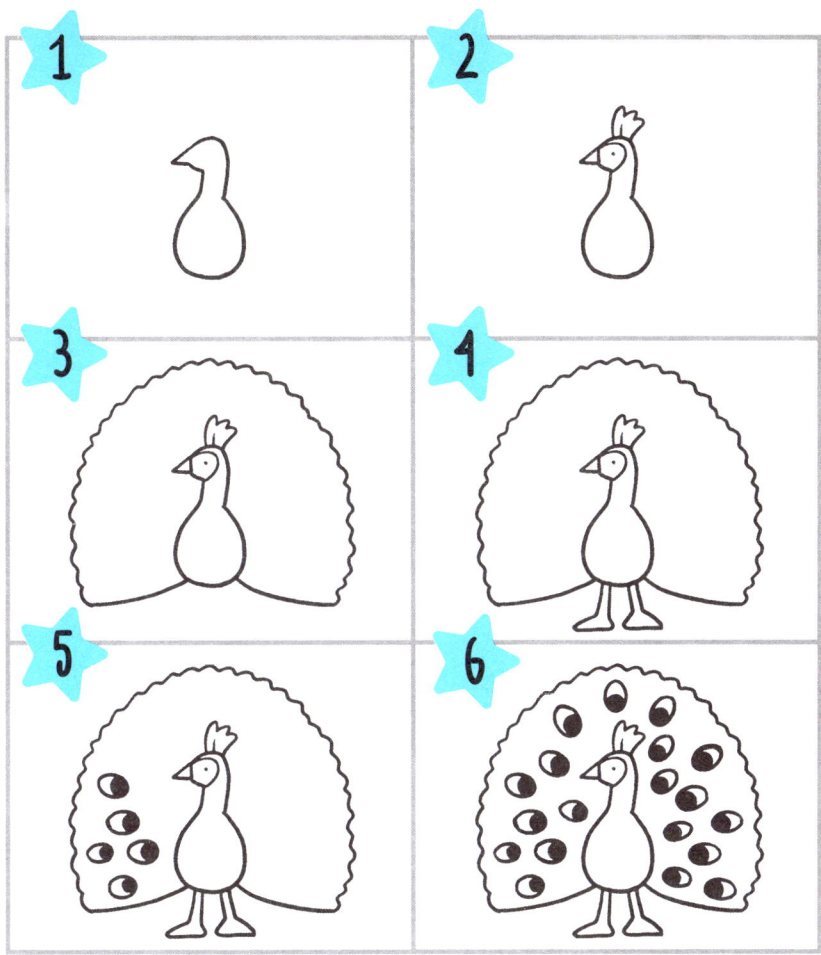

YOUR TURN!

Cute Koalas

Dork facts to amaze your BFs...

⭐ Koalas aren't bears, they are marsupials, like kangaroos and opossums.

⭐ Koalas can be found wherever eucalyptus trees grow.

⭐ When born, a baby koala is carried in its mother's pouch for six months.

⭐ Koalas sleep in the trees during the day — some sleep for up to 18 hours!

⭐ At night, koalas wake to feed on eucalyptus leaves, eating up to two and a half pounds of leaves in a single night!

⭐ Koalas have pouches in their cheeks where they store food for snacks.

 Reasons why I love koalas so much...

_____

_____

_____

_____

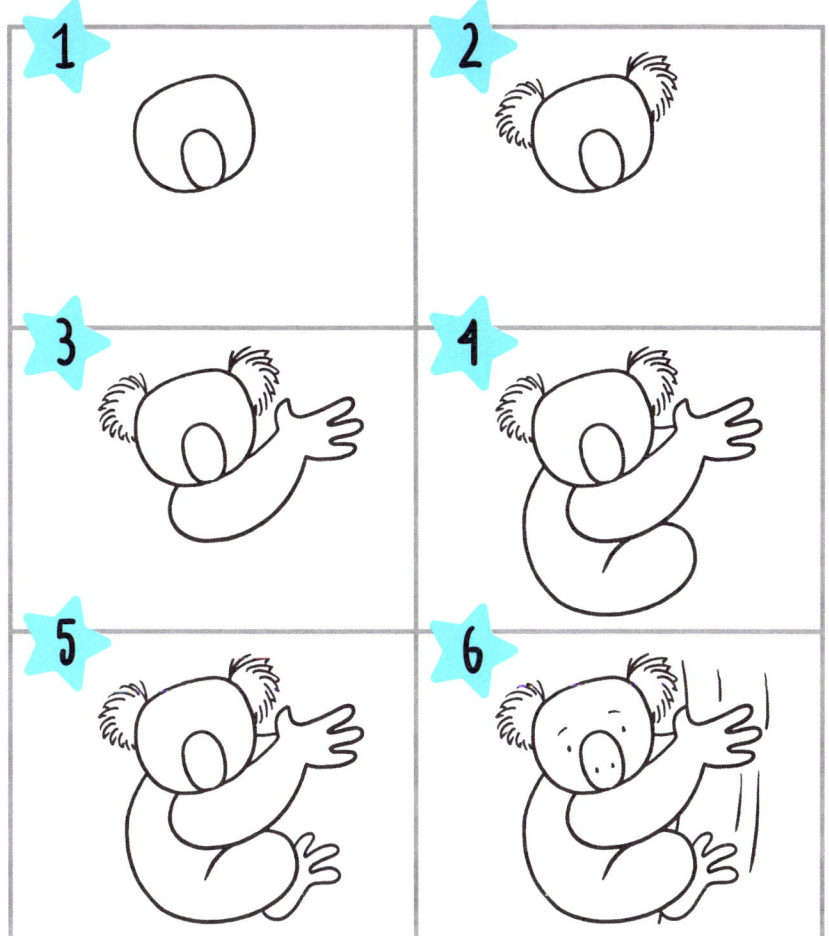

YOUR TURN!

Extraordinary Narwhals

Dork facts to amaze your BFs...

⭐ Narwhals are porpoises. They are related to orcas and dolphins.

⭐ The male narwhal's tusk is actually a tooth that grows through their upper lip and can reach over 10 feet long!

⭐ Narwhals are found in the Arctic ocean around Canada, Russia, Greenland, and Norway.

⭐ Narwhals can grow up to 18 feet long and weigh over 3,500 lbs.

⭐ Narwhals feed on fish and squid. Like orcas and dolphins they usually travel in large groups.

 Reasons why I love narwhals SO much...

_____
_____
_____
_____
_____
_____

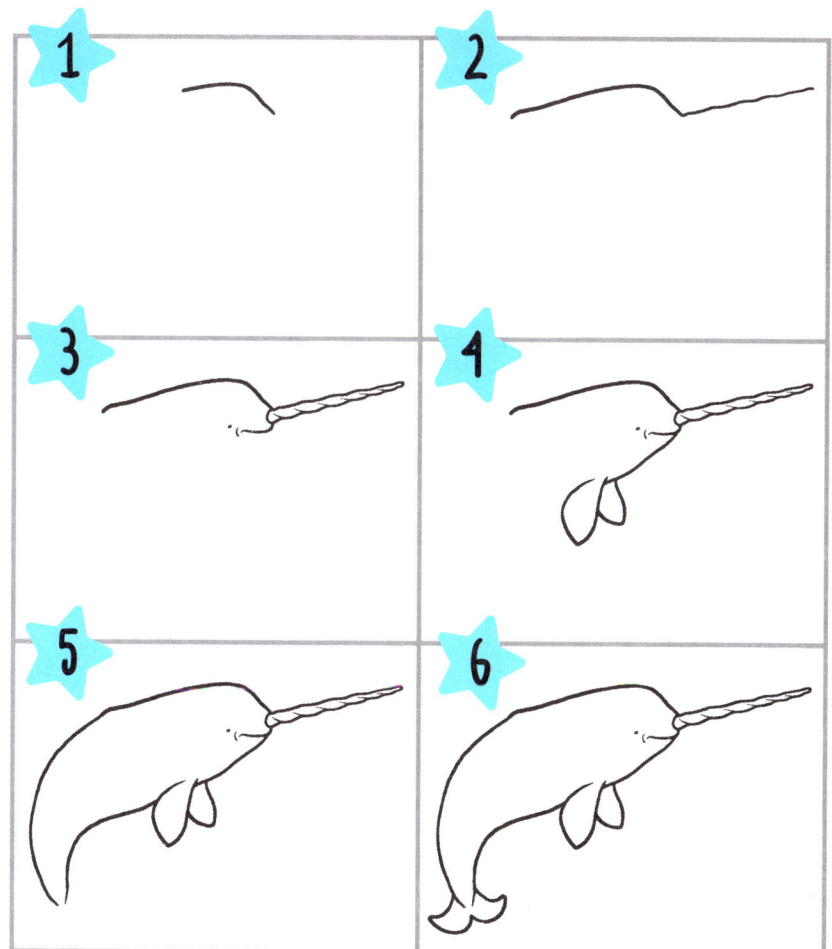

YOUR TURN!

Astonishing Anteaters

Dork facts to amaze your BFs...

⭐ Giant anteaters can measure as long as 6 feet from their nose to the end of their tail!

⭐ Anteaters don't have teeth — they lap up prey with their long tongues before swallowing it whole.

⭐ One anteater can consume as many as 35,000 ants and termites in a day.

⭐ They dig into nests then eat quickly — sometimes for only a minute — before finding another nest to raid.

⭐ Anteaters can be fierce when threatened. They rear up on their hind legs and use their long claws to fight off predators.

 Reasons why I love anteaters so much...

_____
_____
_____
_____

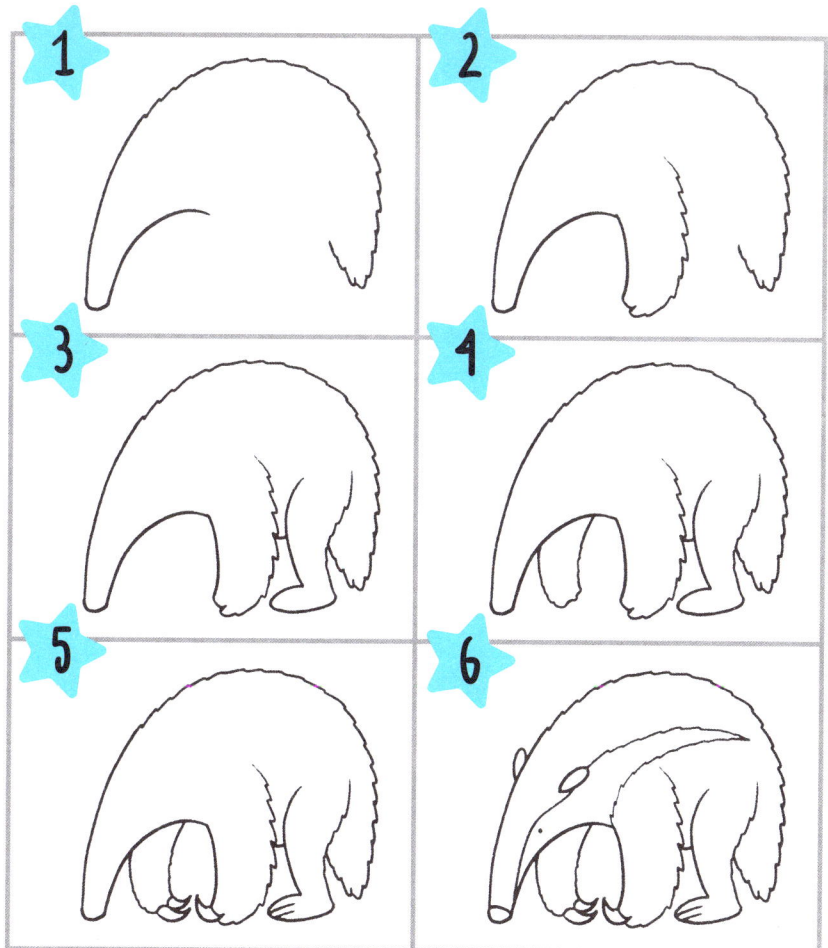

YOUR TURN!

Great Gorillas

Dork facts to amaze your BFs...

⭐ There are two species of gorilla in Africa: the eastern and the western.

⭐ Gorillas are one of the largest and strongest living primates.

⭐ An adult male gorilla can weigh up to 400 pounds and stand nearly 6 feet tall.

⭐ Gorillas eat plants, bamboo shoots, and fruit. Some gorillas also eat ants and termites.

⭐ Gorillas live in families called "troops." Some troops contain three gorillas, some more than 40!

⭐ Gorillas can be very noisy! They bark, hoot, and roar, and also beat their chests to intimidate rivals.

 Reasons why I love gorillas so much...

_____

_____

_____

_____

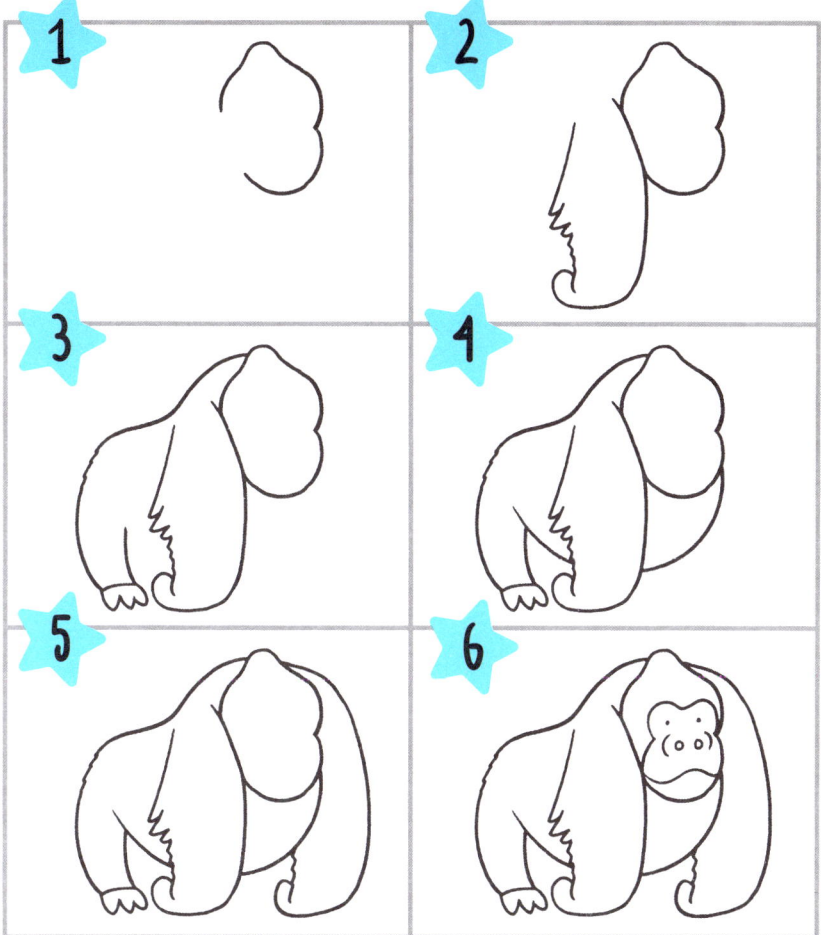

YOUR TURN!

Adorable Axolotls

Dork facts to amaze your Bfs...

⭐ Axolotls are amphibians and part of the salamander family.

⭐ Wild axolotls are only found in lakes and rivers around Mexico City, Mexico.

⭐ Axolotls have distinctive feathery gills on their heads and tadpole-like tails.

⭐ Axolotls are aquatic – they breathe through their gills and also through their skin!

⭐ They have extraordinary healing abilities – if axolotls lose a limb, they can regrow it completely!

 Reasons why I love axolotls SO much...

_____
_____
_____
_____

1
2
3
4
5
6

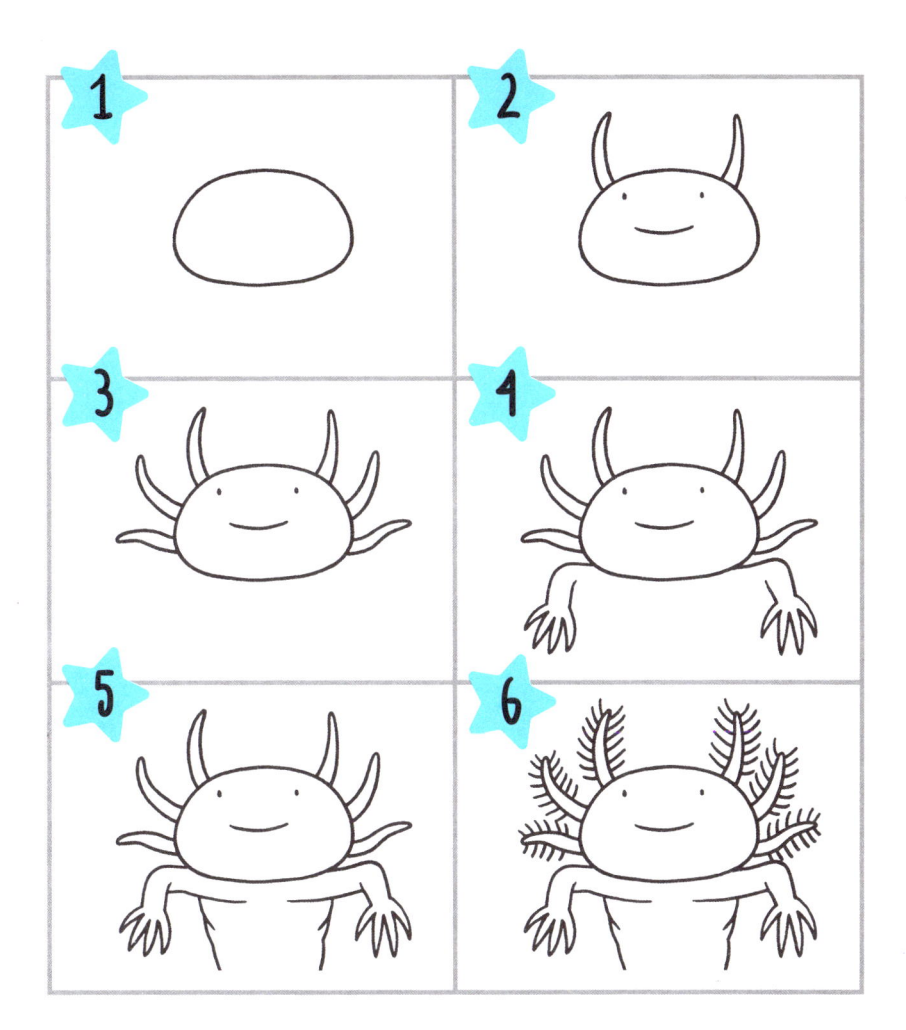

YOUR TURN!

Powerful Rhinos

Dork facts to amaze your BFs...

⭐ Rhinoceros means "nose horn" in Ancient Greek.

⭐ The Javan and Indian rhinos are the only rhinos to have one horn.

⭐ Rhinos use their poo to communicate with other rhinos. Each rhino's poo has a unique smell!

⭐ Despite their size, rhinos are fast and can run at speeds of up to 40 miles per hour.

⭐ In prehistoric times, rhinos had wooly coats! The fluffy Sumatran rhino is the wooly rhino's closest-living relative today.

😍 Reasons why I love rhinos SO much...

_____
_____
_____
_____

1 2 3 4 5 6

YOUR TURN!

Playful Monkeys

Dork facts to amaze your BFs...

⭐ The world's loudest monkey is the howler monkey. Its call can be heard three miles away!

⭐ The largest monkey is the mandrill. It grows to over 2 feet long and weighs up to 100 pounds.

⭐ The pygmy marmoset is the smallest monkey. It weighs less than half a pound and is about the size of a banana!

⭐ New World monkeys are found in Central and South America and Mexico.

⭐ Old World monkeys is the term for monkeys found in Africa and Asia.

😍 Reasons why I love monkeys SO much...

_____
_____
_____
_____
_____

1

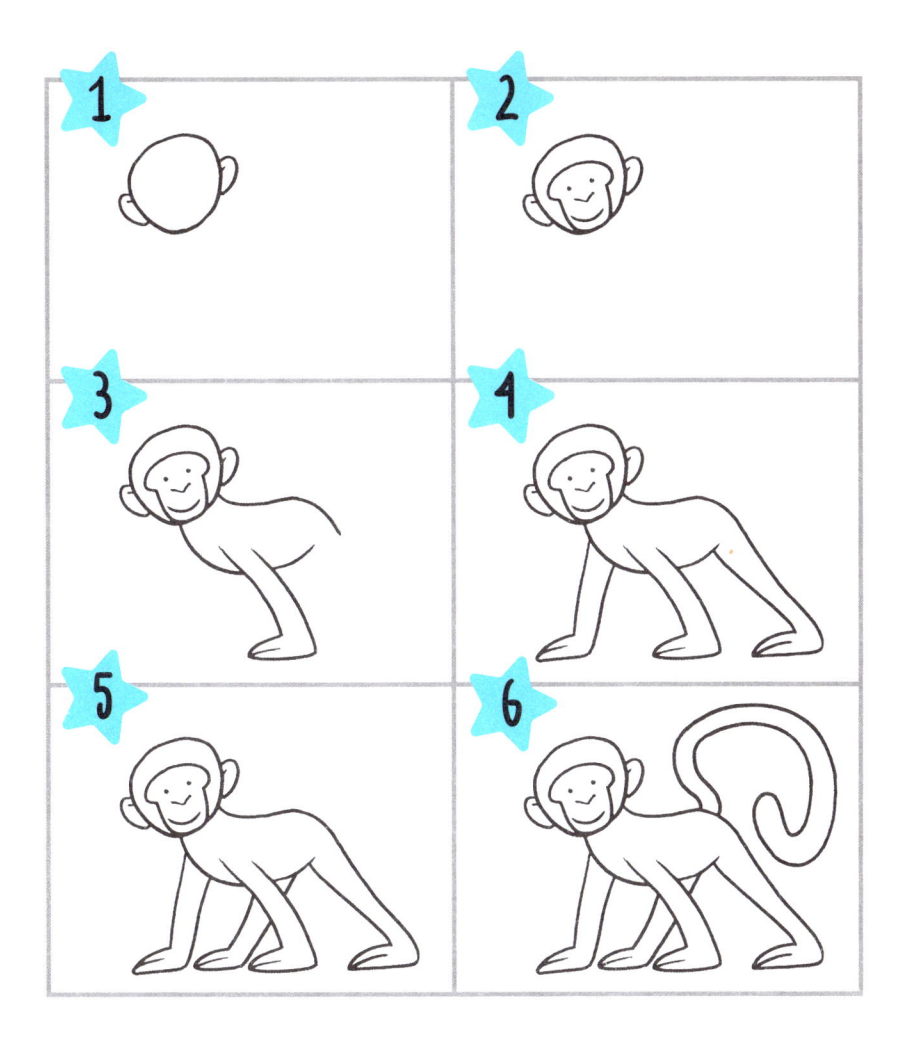

2

3

4

5

6

YOUR TURN!

Noisy Humpback Whales

Dork facts to amaze your BFs...

⭐ Humpback whales are enormous marine mammals growing up to 39-52 feet long, that's as long as a bus!

⭐ Humpbacks are found in coastal waters, where they feed on plankton, krill, and small fish.

⭐ Male humpbacks are noisy. They howl, squeal, whistle, and rumble, sometimes for hours at a time.

⭐ The loud songs are believed to attract females and to communicate with other males.

⭐ Humpbacks are famous for "breeching," where they leap from the water and land with a splash.

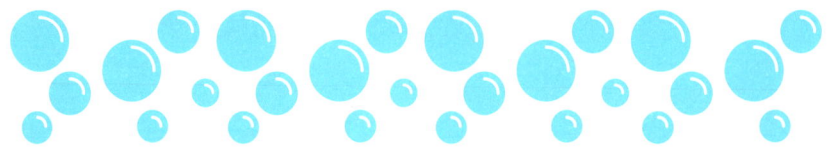

😍 Reasons why I love humpback whales so much...

_____
_____
_____
_____
_____

1
2
3
4
5
6

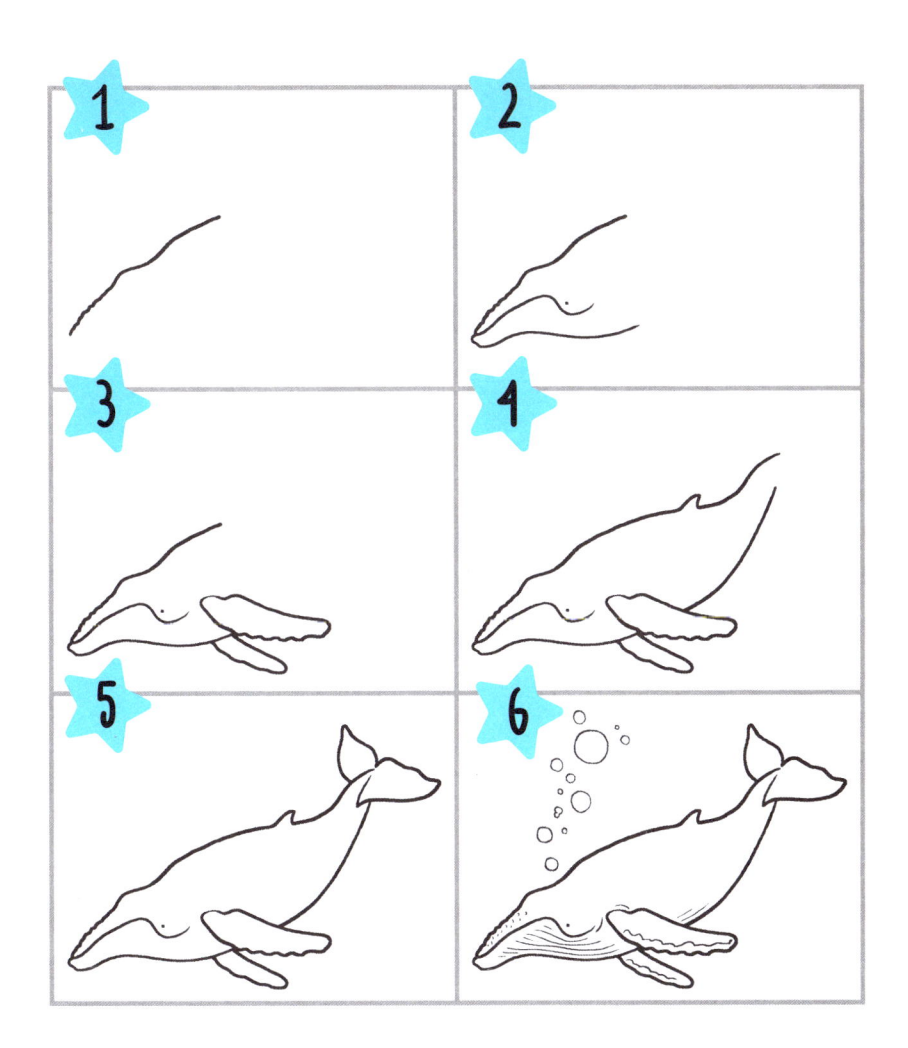

YOUR TURN!

Amazing Orangutans

Dork facts to amaze your BFs...

⭐ Orangutans are found in the tropical rainforests of Sumatra and Borneo, southeast Asia.

⭐ They are well known for their red hair, long, strong arms, and large hands.

⭐ Orangutan means "human of the forest" in Malay.

⭐ Orangutans spend nearly all their lives in trees, swinging from branches in search of food.

⭐ At night, orangutans even sleep up in the trees, in nests made from leaves and branches, away from predators.

😍 Reasons why I love orangutans SO much...

_____
_____
_____
_____
_____
_____

1 **2** **3** **4** **5** **6**

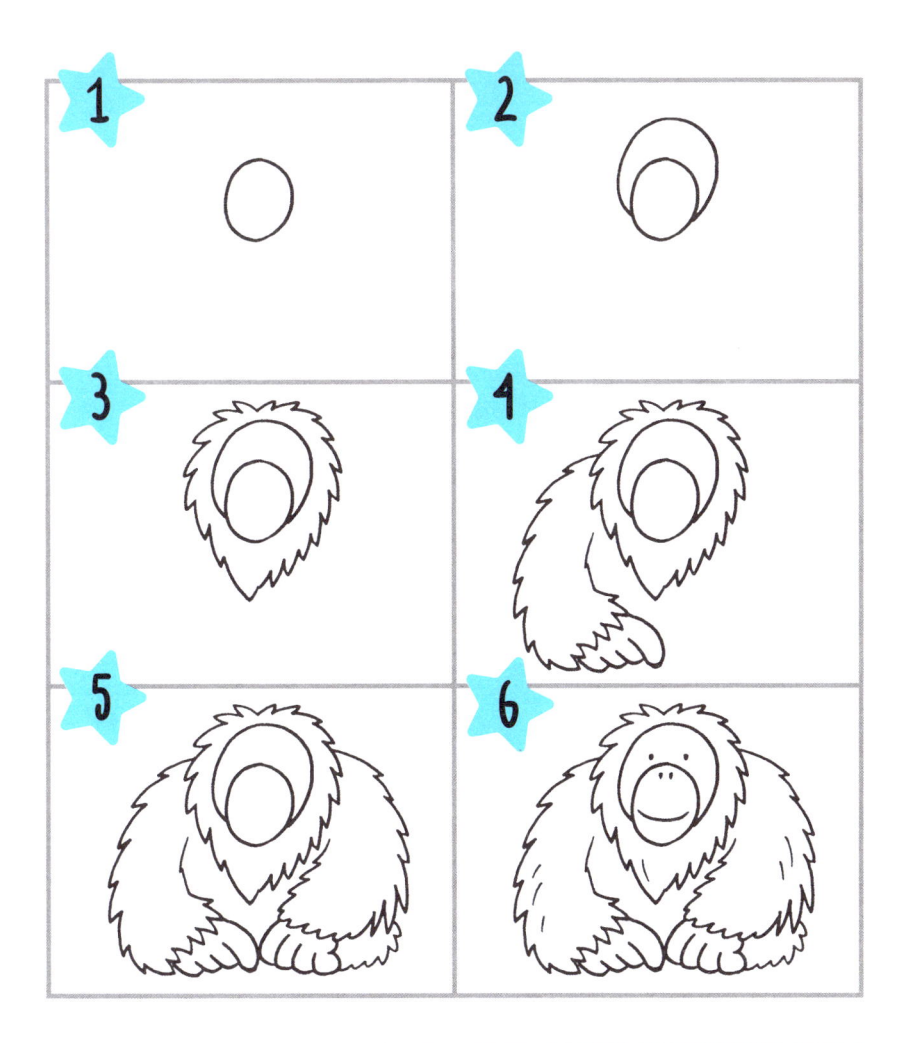

YOUR TURN!

Fantastic Angel Fish

Dork facts to amaze your BFs...

⭐ Queen angel fish are very colorful, with electric blue bodies, bright yellow tails, and flashes of purple and orange on their scales.

⭐ They are found in warm seas around the Caribbean islands and the western Atlantic Ocean.

⭐ Queen angel fish get their name from the blue and black crown-like marking on their heads.

⭐ Their colorful markings help them to blend in against the coral reef, protecting them from predators.

⭐ Queen angel fish feed on sponges, soft coral, algae, and jellyfish.

Reasons why I love angel fish so much...

_____
_____
_____
_____

1

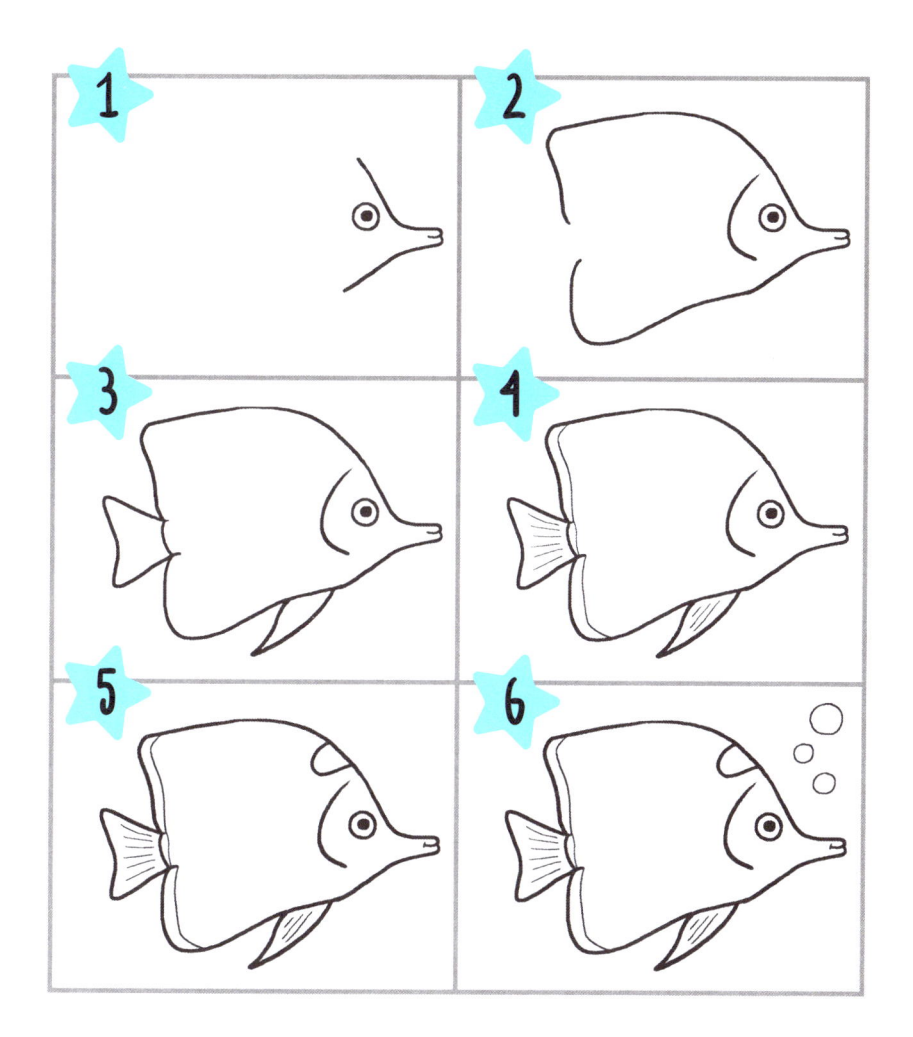

2

3

4

5

6

YOUR TURN!

Use this page to draw some amazing animals! What are they?

What is black and white and eats like a horse?

A zebra!

What's my name?

....

What did the bat say when his friend returned to school?

Welcome bat!

What's my name?

....

What does a sea turtle do on its birthday?

It shell-ebrates!

What's my name?

....

What do polar bears like to eat in the Arctic?

Ice berg-ers!

What's my name?

....

Knock, knock!

Who's there?

Toucan.

Toucan who?

Toucan play at that game!

What's my name?

....

What do you call a lion's reflection?

A copycat!

What's my name?

....

Why did the koala attend college?

Because it had the koala-fications!

What's my name?

....

Why do sharks live in saltwater?

Because pepperwater makes them sneeze!

What's my name?

....

Why was the ocean so friendly?

Because it was always waving!

What's my name?

....

What do you call a well-dressed ant?

eleg-ant!

What's my name?

....

What does a gorilla study at college?

The law of the jungle!

What's my name?

....

What's as big as a rhino but weighs nothing?

Its shadow!

What's my name?

....

Why did the axolotl say moo?

Because it was learning a new language!

What's my name?

....

What do you do with a blue whale?

Make it laugh!

What's my name?

....

What kind of key opens a banana?

A monkey!

What's my name?

....

What's the most musical part of a fish?

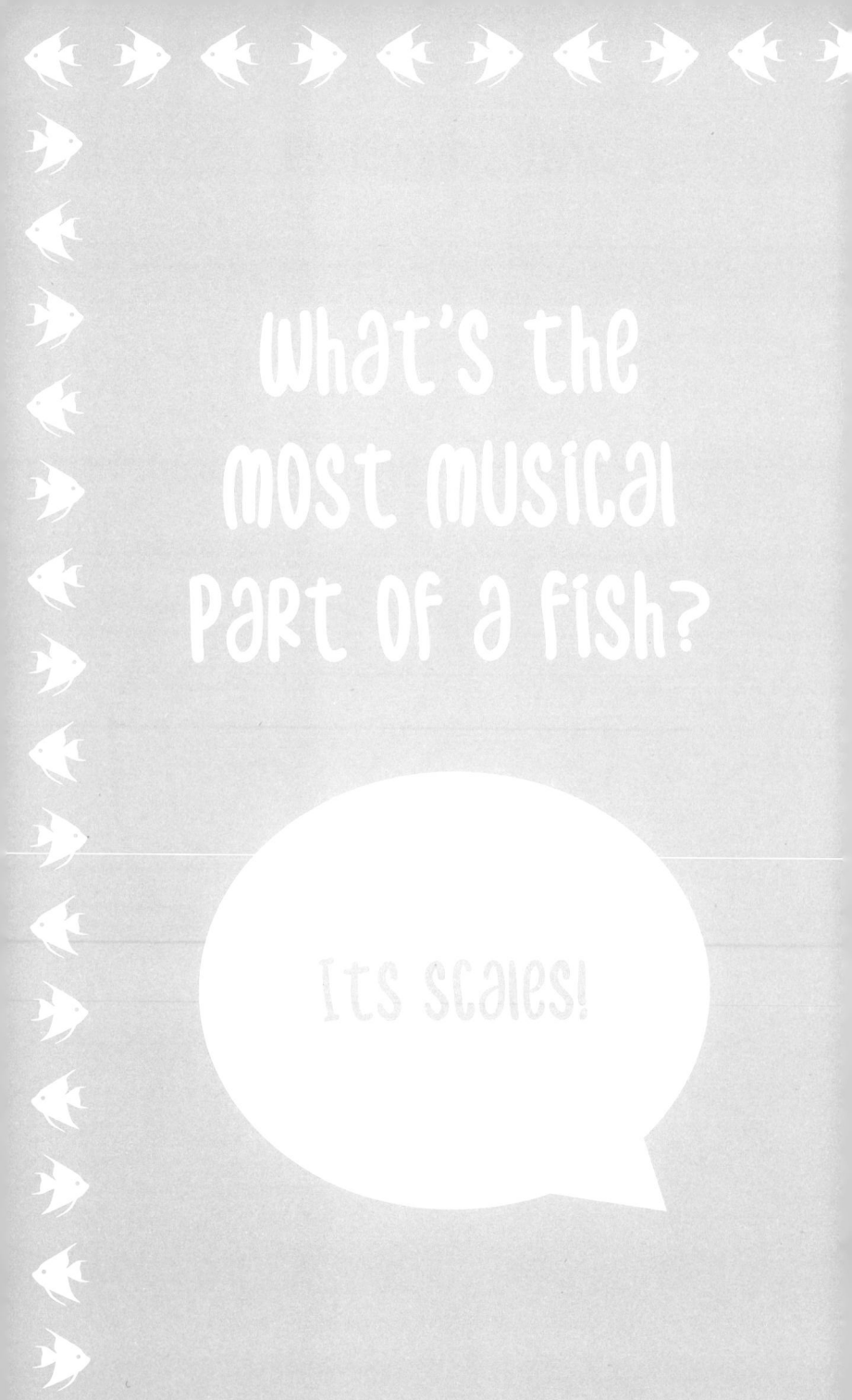

> Its scales!

What's my name?

....

What did
the banana say
to the orangutan?

Nothing! Bananas
don't talk!

What's my name?

....

Write your own amazing animal jokes below!

My paw-some animal sketches...

My paw-some animal sketches...

My paw-some animal sketches...

My paw-some animal sketches...

My Paw-some Animal Sketches...

My paw-some animal sketches...

My paw-some animal sketches...

My paw-some animal sketches...

My paw-some animal sketches...

My paw-some animal sketches...

My paw-some animal sketches...

My paw-some animal sketches...

My paw-some animal sketches...

My paw-some animal sketches...

My paw-some animal sketches...

My paw-some animal sketches...

My paw-some animal sketches...

My paw-some animal sketches...

My paw-some animal sketches...

My Paw-some Animal Sketches...